Lourdes

Prayer Book

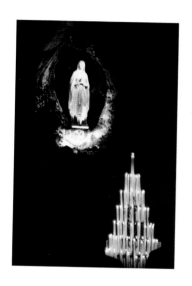

FAMILY PUBLICATIONS · OXFORD

ISBN 978-1-871217-759

published by
Family Publications
6a King Street, Oxford, OX2 6DF
www.familypublications.co.uk

printed in England
through ss media limited

Table of Contents

⁘

*W*hoever opens his or her heart to the Mother encounters and welcomes the Son and is pervaded by his joy. True Marian devotion never obscures or diminishes faith and love for Jesus Christ Our Saviour, the one Mediator between God and humankind.

On the contrary, entrustment to Our Lady is a privileged path, tested by numerous saints, for a more faithful following of the Lord. Consequently, let us entrust ourselves to her with filial abandonment! ...

May the motherly intercession of the Queen of Saints obtain for all Christ's disciples the gift of an unwavering faith and an unswerving Gospel witness.

Pope Benedict XVI, May 31 2006

Introduction

LOURDES

Who could have predicted, 150 years ago, that the name of this little town in the Pyrenees would become world famous? Yet Our Lady chose this place to appear on eighteen occasions from 11 February to 16 July 1858 to Bernadette Soubirous, a local uneducated teenager. The beautiful lady gave her name in the girl's dialect, "*Que soy era Immaculada Concepciou*", thus confirming the Marian dogma of the Immaculate Conception proclaimed a few years before, in 1854.

Since then, crowds of pilgrims – especially sick and disabled people of all conditions – have been flocking to Lourdes, bringing to the grotto of Massabielle their prayer intentions, their worries, the well-being of their loved ones. Kneeling privately in front of the statue of Our Lady or gathered together with hundreds of others to say the Rosary on the meadow, or else processing with candlelights around the sanctuary, they repeat prayers to Mary, quietly conversing with their heavenly Mother or singing to her in loving praise.

This booklet, illustrated with pictures taken at Lourdes, offers a wide range of the most popular prayers and devotions to the Blessed Virgin. The original idea for this prayer book was inspired by Father Brian Taylor, priest-in-charge at the Catholic Parish of St Edward the Confessor in Sutton Park, Guildford, to whom the publishers are grateful.

Pope John Paul II's Prayer to Our Lady of Lourdes
(August 15 2004)

❧

*H*ail Mary, poor and humble woman,
Blessed by the Most High!
Virgin of hope, dawn of a new era,
We join in your song of praise,
to celebrate the Lord's mercy,
to proclaim the coming of the Kingdom
and the full liberation of humanity.

Hail Mary, lowly handmaid of the Lord,
   Glorious Mother of Christ!
   Faithful Virgin, holy dwelling-place of the Word,
   Teach us to persevere in listening to the Word,
   and to be docile to the voice of the Spirit,
   attentive to his promptings
   in the depths of our conscience
   and to his manifestations in the events of history.

Hail Mary, woman of sorrows,
   Mother of the living!
   Virgin spouse beneath the Cross, the new Eve,
   Be our guide along the paths of the world.
   Teach us to experience and to spread the love of Christ,
   to stand with you before the innumerable crosses
   on which your Son is still crucified.

Hail Mary, woman of faith,
   First of the disciples!
   Virgin Mother of the Church,
   help us always to account for the hope that is in us,
   with trust in human goodness and the Father's love.
   Teach us to build up the world beginning from within:
   in the depths of silence and prayer,
   in the joy of fraternal love,
   in the unique fruitfulness of the Cross.

Holy Mary, Mother of believers,
   Our Lady of Lourdes,
   pray for us.
                        Amen

Our Lady of Lourdes

❧

*E*ver Immaculate Virgin,
   Mother of mercy,
   health of the sick,
   refuge of sinners,
   comfort of the afflicted,
   you know my needs, my troubles, my sufferings;
   cast on me a look of pity.
   By appearing in the grotto of Lourdes,
   you were pleased to make it a privileged sanctuary,
   from which you dispense your favours,
   and already many sufferers have obtained the cure
   of their infirmities,
   both spiritual and physical.
   I come, therefore, with the most unbounded confidence
   to implore your maternal intercession.
   Obtain most loving mother, my requests,
   through Jesus Christ your Son our Lord.
   I will endeavour to imitate your virtues,
   that I may one day share your glory
   and bless you in eternity.

Amen

Prayer to Our Lady of Lourdes

*O*Holy Virgin,
in the midst of your days of glory,
do not forget the sorrows of this earth.
Cast a merciful glance upon those who are suffering,
struggling against difficulties, with their lips
constantly pressed against life's bitter cup.
Have pity on those who love each other and are separated.
Have pity on our rebellious hearts.
Have pity on our weak faith.
Have pity on those who weep,
on those who pray, on those who fear.
Grant hope and peace to all.

Amen

Kontakion of the Annunciation

From the Catholic Byzantine rite

I am your own, O Mother of God!
To you, Protectress and Leader,
My songs of victory!
To you who saved me from danger,
My hymn of thanksgiving!
In your invincible might, Deliver me from all danger,
That I may sing to you:
"Hail, O Bride and Maiden ever-pure!"

Prayers by Saint Bernadette

✧✧

*H*ow happy my soul was, good Mother, when I had the good fortune to gaze upon you! How I love to recall the pleasant moments spent under your gaze, so full of kindness and mercy for us. Yes, tender Mother, you stooped down to earth to appear to a mere child.

You, the Queen of Heaven and Earth, chose to use what is weakest in the eyes of men. O Mary, give the precious virtue of humility to she who dares to call herself your child. O loving Mother, help your child resemble you in everything and in every way. In a word, grant that I may be a child according to your heart and the heart of your dear Son.

———•—•———

*L*et the crucifix be not only in my eyes and on my breast, but in my heart. O Jesus! Release all my affections and draw them upwards. Let my crucified heart sink forever into Thine and bury itself in the mysterious wound made by the entry of the lance.

———•—•———

*O*my God, I beg You, by Your loneliness, not that You may spare me affliction, but that You may not abandon me in it. When I encounter affliction, teach me to see You in it as my sole Comforter. Let affliction strengthen my faith, fortify my hope, and purify my love. Grant me the grace to see Your Hand in my affliction, and to desire no other comforter but You.

Amen

Prayers to Saint Bernadette

❦❦❦

*S*aint Bernadette, little shepherdess of Lourdes favoured with eighteen apparitions of the Immaculate Virgin Mary and with the privilege of lovingly conversing with her, now that you are eternally enjoying the entrancing beauty of the Immaculate Mother of God, do not forsake me your devoted supplicant, who am still in the valley of tears.

Intercede for me that I too may walk the simple paths of faith. Help me to imitate your example, at our heavenly Queen's request, by saying the Rosary daily and by doing penance for sinners. Teach me to imitate your wonderful devotedness to God and Our Lady the Immaculate Conception so that, like you, I may be blessed with the grace of lasting faithfulness and enjoy the happiness in heaven of the eternal vision of God the Father, Son and Holy Spirit.

———•◦•———

O Saint Bernadette, who, as a meek and pure child, did eighteen times at Lourdes contemplate the beauty of the Immaculate Mother of God and received her messages, and who afterwards wished to hide yourself from the world in the convent of Nevers, and to offer yourself there as a victim for the conversion of sinners, obtain for us the grace of purity, simplicity and mortification that we also may attain to the vision of God and of Mary in Heaven.

Amen

Prayer to Our Lady of Lourdes

Venerable Pope Pius XII

❧❧

*I*mmaculate Virgin of Lourdes,
in compliance with your loving invitation, we kneel
before you in the lowly grotto where you appeared
in order to point out the way of prayer and penance
to those who had strayed and to distribute to those
sorely beset by bitter anguish the graces and marvels
of your queenly bounty. Accept, compassionate Queen,
the praise and prayers which all peoples and nations
address to you with confidence.

O shining vision of Paradise, dispel the shadows of
error from our minds with the light of Faith.
O mystical Rose, comfort dejected souls with the
heavenly fragrance of Hope.
O inexhaustible source of life-giving waters, refresh
our barren hearts with the waves of Divine Love.

Grant that we, your children, strengthened in affliction,
protected in danger, supported in our struggles, may
so love and serve your Divine Son as to merit eternal
joys at the foot of your Heavenly throne.

Amen

Ave Maria

Ave Maria, gratia plena, Dominus tecum.
  Benedicta tu in mulieribus,
  et benedictus fructus ventris tui, Iesus.
  Sancta Maria, Mater Dei,
  ora pro nobis peccatoribus,
  nunc et in hora mortis nostrae.

Amen

*H*ail Mary
  Full of Grace,
  The Lord is with thee.
  Blessed art thou among women,
  and blessed is the fruit of thy womb, Jesus.
  Holy Mary, Mother of God,
  pray for us sinners now,
  and at the hour of our death.

Amen

The Angelus

✎✎

V. The Angel of the Lord declared unto Mary,
R. And she conceived of the Holy Spirit.

Hail Mary, full of grace, the Lord is with thee. Blessed art thou
among women and blessed is the fruit of thy womb, Jesus.

Holy Mary, Mother of God, pray for us sinners, now,
and at the hour of our death. Amen

V. Behold the handmaid of the Lord,
R. Be it done unto me according to Thy word.

Hail Mary, ...

V. And the Word was made flesh,
R. And dwelt among us.

Hail Mary, ...

V. Pray for us, O holy Mother of God,
R. That we may be made worthy of the promises of Christ.

Let us pray

Pour forth, we beseech Thee, O Lord, Thy grace into our hearts;
that we, to whom the Incarnation of Christ Thy Son was made
known by the message of an Angel, may, by His Passion and
Cross, be brought to the glory of His Resurrection. Through
the same Christ our Lord.

Amen

Magnificat

*M*agnificat anima mea Dominum
Et exultavit spiritus meus in Deo salutari meo.
Quia respexit humilitatem ancillæ suæ:
ecce enim ex hoc beatam me dicent omnes generationes.
Quia fecit mihi magna qui potens est, et sanctum nomen eius.
Et misericordia eius a progenie in progenies timentibus eum.
Fecit potentiam in brachio suo,
dispersit superbos mente cordis sui.
Deposuit potentes de sede et exaltavit humiles.
Esurientes implevit bonis et divites dimisit inanes,
Suscepit Israel puerum suum recordatus misericordiæ suæ,
Sicut locutus est ad patres nostros,
Abraham et semini eius in sæcula.

*M*y soul glorifies the Lord,
my spirit rejoices in God, my Saviour.
He looks on his servant in her lowliness;
henceforth all ages will call me blessed.
The Almighty works marvels for me. Holy his Name!
His mercy is from age to age, on those who fear him.
He puts forth his arm in strength
and scatters the proud-hearted.
He casts the mighty from their thrones and raises the lowly.
He fills the starving with good things,
sends the rich away empty.
He protects Israel, his servant, remembering his mercy,
the mercy promised to our fathers,
to Abraham and his sons for ever.

Alma Redemptoris Mater
(11th century)

*A*lma Redemptoris Mater, quae pervia caeli
Porta manes, et stella maris, succurre cadenti,
Surgere qui curat, populo: tu quae genuisti,
Natura mirante, tuum sanctum Genitorem
Virgo prius ac posterius, Gabrielis ab ore
Sumens illud Ave, peccatorum miserere.

---

*L*oving Mother of our Saviour, Hear thou thy people's cry
Star of the deep and Portal of the sky!
Mother of Him who thee from nothing made.
Sinking we strive and call to thee for aid:
Oh, by that joy which Gabriel brought to thee,
Thou Virgin first and last, let us thy mercy see.

Salve Regina

(c. 11th century)

❧❧

*S*alve Regina, Mater misericordiae,
vita, dulcedo, et spes nostra, salve.
Ad te clamamus, exsules filii Evae,
ad te suspiramus, gementes et flentes
in hac lacrimarum valle.
Eia, ergo, advocata nostra, illos tuos
misericordes oculos ad nos converte;
et Jesum, benedictum fructum ventris tui,
nobis post hoc exilium ostende.
O clemens, O pia, O dulcis Virgo Maria.

———•••———

*H*ail Holy Queen, Mother of mercy,
Hail our life, our sweetness, and our hope.
To thee do we cry, poor banished children of Eve.
To thee do we send up our sighs
mourning and weeping in this vale of tears.
Turn then, most gracious advocate,
thine eyes of mercy towards us,
and after this our exile show unto us
the blessed fruit of thy womb, Jesus.
O clement, O loving, O sweet Virgin Mary.

V. Pray for us, O holy Mother of God.
R. That we may be made worthy of the promises of Christ.

Ave, Regina Caelorum
(12th century)

❧

*A*ve, Regina caelorum,
  Ave, Domina Angelorum:
  Salve, radix, salve, porta
  Ex qua mundo lux est orta:

  Gaude, Virgo gloriosa,
  Super omnes speciosa,
  Vale, o valde decora,
  Et pro nobis Christum exora.

*H*ail, O Queen of Heaven.
  Hail, O Lady of Angels
  Hail! thou root, hail! thou gate
  From whom unto the world, a light has arisen:

  Rejoice, O glorious Virgin,
  Lovely beyond all others,
  Farewell, most beautiful maiden,
  And pray for us to Christ.

V. Allow me to praise thee, O sacred Virgin.
R. Against thy enemies give me strength.

Let us pray

Grant, O merciful God, to our weak natures Thy protection,
that we who commemorate the holy Mother of God may,
by the help of her intercession, arise from our iniquities.
Through the same Christ our Lord.   Amen

Regina Caeli

(c. 10th century)

❧

*R*egina caeli, laetare, alleluia:
Quia quem meruisti portare, alleluia,
Resurrexit, sicut dixit, alleluia.
Ora pro nobis Deum, alleluia.

V. Gaude et laetare, Virgo Maria, alleluia.
R. Quia surrexit Dominus vere, alleluia.

———————

*Q*ueen of heaven, rejoice, alleluia:
For He whom you did merit to bear, alleluia,
Has risen, as He said, alleluia.
Pray for us to God, alleluia.

V. Rejoice and be glad, O Virgin Mary, alleluia.
R. For the Lord has truly risen, alleluia.

Let us pray

O God, who gave joy to the world through the resurrection of your Son, our Lord Jesus Christ, grant we beseech you, that through the intercession of the Virgin Mary, His Mother, we may obtain the joys of everlasting life. Through the same Christ our Lord.

Amen

The Memorare
(17th century)

❧⟡❧

*R*emember, O most loving Virgin Mary,
  that it is a thing unheard of,
  that anyone ever had recourse to your protection,
  implored your help, or sought your intercession,
  and was left forsaken.
  Filled therefore with confidence in your goodness
  I fly to you, O Mother, Virgin of virgins.
  To you I come, before you I stand,
  a sorrowful sinner.
  Despise not my poor words,
  O Mother of the Word of God,
  but graciously hear and grant my prayer.

Amen

Litany of Our Lady of Lourdes

Lord have mercy,
Lord have mercy.
Christ have mercy,
Christ have mercy.
Lord have mercy,
Lord have mercy.
Christ hear us,
Christ graciously hear us.
God the Father of Heaven,
have mercy on us.
God the Son, Redeemer of the world,
have mercy on us.
God the Holy Spirit,
have mercy on us.
Holy Trinity, one God,
have mercy on us.

Holy Mary, *pray for us.*
Holy Mother of God, *pray for us.*
Mother of Christ, *pray for us.*
Mother of our Saviour, *pray for us.*
Our Lady of Lourdes, help of Christians, *pray for us.*
Our Lady of Lourdes, source of love, *pray for us.*
Our Lady of Lourdes, mother of the poor, *pray for us.*
Our Lady of Lourdes, mother of the handicapped, *pray for us.*
Our Lady of Lourdes, mother of orphans, *pray for us.*
Our Lady of Lourdes, mother of all children, *pray for us.*
Our Lady of Lourdes, mother of all nations, *pray for us.*
Our Lady of Lourdes, mother of the Church, *pray for us.*

Our Lady of Lourdes, friend of the lonely, *pray for us.*
Our Lady of Lourdes, comforter of those who mourn, *pray for us.*
Our Lady of Lourdes, shelter of the homeless, *pray for us.*
Our Lady of Lourdes, guide of travellers, *pray for us.*
Our Lady of Lourdes, strength of the weak, *pray for us.*
Our Lady of Lourdes, refuge of sinners, *pray for us.*
Our Lady of Lourdes, comforter of the suffering, *pray for us.*
Our Lady of Lourdes, help of the dying, *pray for us.*
Queen of heaven, *pray for us.*
Queen of peace, *pray for us.*

Lamb of God, you take away the sins of the world,
   spare us O Lord.
Lamb of God, you take away the sins of the world,
   graciously hear us, O Lord.
Lamb of God, you take away the sins of the world,
   have mercy on us.
Christ hear us,
   Christ graciously hear us.

Let us pray
   Grant us, your servants, we pray you, Lord God, to enjoy perpetual health of mind and body. By the glorious intercession of Blessed Mary ever Virgin, may we be delivered from present sorrows, and enjoy everlasting happiness. Through Christ our Lord.

Amen

Immaculate Mary

ক৩৵

Immaculate Mary!
Our hearts are on fire,
That title so wondrous
Fills all our desire.

Ave, ave, ave, Maria! (2)

We pray for God's glory,
May His Kingdom come!
We pray for His Vicar,
Our Father, and Rome.

Ave ...

We pray for our Mother
The Church upon earth,
And bless, sweetest Lady,
The land of our birth.

Ave ...

For poor, sick, afflicted
thy mercy we crave;
and comfort the dying
thou light of the grave.

Ave ...

There is no need, Mary,
nor ever has been,
which thou canst not succour,
Immaculate Queen.

Ave ...

In grief and temptation,
in joy or in pain,
we'll ask thee, our Mother,
nor seek thee in vain.

Ave ...

O bless us, dear Lady,
With blessings from heaven.
And to our petitions
Let answer be given.

Ave ...

In death's solemn moment,
our Mother, be nigh;
as children of Mary
O teach us to die.

Ave ...

And crown thy sweet mercy
With this special grace,
To behold soon in heaven
God's ravishing face.

Ave ...

Now to God be all glory
And worship for aye,
And to God's virgin Mother
An endless Ave.

Ave ...

Tota Pulchra es

(4th century)

❧

Tota pulchra es, Maria
   et macula originalis non est in te.
   Vestimentum tuum candidum quasi nix,
      et facies tua sicut sol.
   Tota pulchra es, Maria
      et macula originalis non est in te.
   Tu gloria Jerusalem, tu laetitia Israel,
      tu honorificentia populi nostri.
   Tota pulchra es, Maria.

———•———

You are completely pure, Mary,
   and the stain of original sin is not within you.
   Your clothing is white like snow,
      and your face is like the sun.
   You are completely pure, Mary,
      and the stain of original sin is not within you.
   You are the glory of Jerusalem, you are the joy of Israel,
      you are the honoured of our people.
   You are completely pure, Mary.

O Virgin Immaculate

St Ephraem of Edessa, 4th century

*O*Virgin Immaculate,
Mother of God and my Mother,
from your sublime heights
turn your eyes of pity on me.
Filled with confidence in your goodness
and knowing full well your power,
I beg you to extend to me your assistance
in the journey of life, which is
so full of dangers for my soul.
In order that I may never be
a slave of the devil through sin,
but may ever live with my heart humble and pure,
I entrust myself wholly to you.
I consecrate my heart to you forever,
my only desire being to love your divine Son, Jesus.
Mary, none of your devout servants has ever perished;
may I, too, be saved.

Amen

Sub tuum Praesidium

(3rd century)

❧

Sub tuum praesidium confugimus,
Sancta Dei Genetrix.
Nostras deprecationes ne despicias
in necessitatibus nostris,
sed a periculis cunctis
libera nos semper,
Virgo gloriosa et benedicta.

Amen

———◆———

We fly to thy protection,
O holy Mother of God;
despise not our petitions
in our necessities,
but deliver us always
from all dangers,
O glorious and blessed Virgin.

Amen

Prayer to Our Mother of Sorrows

Our mother of sorrows,
with strength from above you stood by the cross,
sharing in the sufferings of Jesus,
and with tender care
you bore Him in your arms, mourning and weeping.

We praise you for your faith,
which accepted the life God planned for you.
We praise you for your hope,
which trusted that God would do great things in you.
We praise you for your love
in bearing with Jesus the sorrows of His passion.

Holy Mary,
may we follow your example,
and stand by all your children
who need comfort and love.

Mother of God,
stand by us in our trials
and care for us in our many needs.
Pray for us now and at the hour of our death.

Amen

Prayer to Our Lady of Mercy

St Augustine of Hippo, 5th century

∽∂∾

*B*lessed Virgin Mary,
who can worthily repay you with praise and thanks
for having rescued a fallen world
by your generous consent!
Receive our gratitude,
and by your prayers obtain the pardon of our sins.
Take our prayers into the sanctuary of heaven
and enable them to make our peace with God.

Holy Mary, help the miserable,
strengthen the discouraged,
comfort the sorrowful,
pray for your people,
plead for the clergy,
intercede for all women consecrated to God.
May all who venerate you
feel now your help and protection.
Be ready to help us when we pray,
and bring back to us the answers to our prayers.
Make it your continual concern
to pray for the people of God,
for you were blessed by God
and were made worthy to bear
the Redeemer of the world,
who lives and reigns forever.

Amen

Prayer for Life

Pope John Paul II

❧❧

O Mary, bright dawn of the new world, Mother of the living, to you we entrust the cause of life.

Look down, O Mother, on the vast numbers of babies not allowed to be born, of the poor whose lives are made difficult, of men and women who are victims of brutal violence, of the elderly and the sick killed by indifference or out of misguided mercy.

Grant that all who believe in your Son may proclaim the Gospel of life with honesty and love to the people of our time.

Obtain for them the grace to accept that Gospel as a gift ever new, the joy of celebrating it with gratitude throughout their lives and the courage to bear witness to it resolutely, in order to build, together with all people of good will, a civilisation of truth and love, to the praise and glory of God, the Creator and lover of life.

Amen

Prayer by Pope Benedict XVI

Deus Caritas Est, §42

*H*oly Mary, Mother of God,
you have given the world its true light,
Jesus, your Son – the Son of God.
You abandoned yourself completely
to God's call and thus became a wellspring
of the goodness which flows forth from him.
Show us Jesus. Lead us to him.
Teach us to know and love him,
so that we too can become
capable of true love
and be fountains of living water
in the midst of a thirsting world.

Ave Maris Stella
(9th century)

Hail, thou Star of ocean,
Portal of the sky!
Ever Virgin Mother
Of the Lord most high!

Oh! by Gabriel's Ave,
Uttered long ago,
Eva's name reversing,
Establish peace below.

Break the captives' fetters;
Light on blindness pour;
All our ills expelling,
Every bliss implore.

Show thyself a Mother;
Offer Him our sighs,
Who for us Incarnate
Did not thee despise.

Virgin of all virgins!
To thy shelter take us:
Gentlest of the gentle!
Chaste and gentle make us.

Still, as on we journey,
Help our weak endeavour;
Till with thee and Jesus
We rejoice forever.

Through the highest heaven,
To the Almighty Three,
Father, Son, and Spirit,
One same glory be.

                    Amen

Litany of the Blessed Virgin Mary

Lord, have mercy, *Lord, have mercy.*
Christ, have mercy, *Christ, have mercy.*
Lord, have mercy, *Lord, have mercy.*
Christ, hear us, *Christ, graciously hear us.*

God the Father of heaven,
 have mercy on us.
God the Son, Redeemer of the World,
 have mercy on us.
God the Holy Spirit,
 have mercy on us.
Holy Trinity, one God,
 have mercy on us.

  Holy Mary, *pray for us.*
  Holy Mother of God, *pray for us.*
  Holy Virgin of virgins, ...
  Mother of Christ, ...
  Mother of Divine Grace, ...
  Mother most pure, ...
  Mother most chaste, ...
  Mother inviolate, ...
  Mother undefiled, ...
  Mother most lovable, ...
  Mother most admirable, ...
  Mother of good counsel, ...
  Mother of our Creator, ...
  Mother of our Saviour, ...

Virgin most prudent, *pray for us*.
Virgin most venerable, ...
Virgin most renowned, ...
Virgin most powerful, ...
Virgin most merciful, ...
Virgin most faithful, ...
Mirror of justice, ...
Seat of wisdom, ...
Cause of our joy, ...
Spiritual vessel, ...
Vessel of honour, ...
Singular vessel of devotion, ...
Mystical rose, ...
Tower of David, ...
Tower of ivory, ...
House of gold, ...
Ark of the covenant, ...
Gate of heaven, ...
Morning star, ...
Health of the sick, ...
Refuge of sinners, ...
Comfort of the afflicted, ...
Help of Christians, ...
Queen of Angels, ...
Queen of Patriarchs, ...
Queen of Prophets, ...

Queen of Apostles, *pray for us.*
Queen of Martyrs, ...
Queen of Confessors, ...
Queen of Virgins, ...
Queen of all Saints, ...
Queen conceived without original sin, ...
Queen assumed into heaven, ...
Queen of the most holy Rosary, ...
Queen of Peace, ...

Lamb of God, you take away the sins of the world,
   spare us, O Lord,
Lamb of God, you take away the sins of the world,
   graciously hear us, O Lord,
Lamb of God, you take away the sins of the world,
   have mercy on us.

Let us pray

Grant we beseech Thee, O Lord God, that we, Thy servants, may enjoy perpetual health of mind and body: and, by the glorious intercession of the blessed Mary, ever Virgin, be delivered from present sorrow and enjoy eternal happiness. Through Christ, our Lord.

Amen

The Mysteries of the Rosary

෨ઌ

The Joyful Mysteries

1. The Annunciation (Lk 1:26-38).
2. The Visitation (Lk 1:39-45).
3. The Nativity (Lk 2:1-7).
4. The Presentation in the Temple (Lk 2:22-35).
5. The Finding of the Child Jesus in the Temple (Lk 2:41-52).

The Luminous Mysteries

1. The Baptism of Christ in the Jordan (Mt 3:13-17).
2. The Wedding Feast at Cana (Jn 2:1-12).
3. The Proclamation of the Kingdom (Mk 1:14-15; 2:3-12).
4. The Transfiguration (Lk 9:28-36).
5. The Institution of the Eucharist (Mt 26:26-29).

The Sorrowful Mysteries

1. The Agony of Christ in the Garden (Mk 14:32-42).
2. The Scourging at the Pillar (Mt 27:15-26).
3. The Crowning with Thorns (Mt 27:27-31).
4. The Carrying of the Cross (Jn 19:15-17; Lk 23:27-32).
5. The Crucifixion of Jesus (Lk 23:33-38, 44-46).

The Glorious Mysteries

1. The Resurrection of Jesus (Mt 28:1-8).
2. The Ascension of Jesus into Heaven (Ac 1:6-11).
3. The Descent of the Holy Spirit (Ac 2:1-12).
4. The Assumption of Mary into Heaven (1 Th 4:13-18).
5. The Coronation of Our Lady in Heaven (Rev 12:1; 14:1-5).

Consecration to Our Lady

❧❧

*T*his day, with the whole court of heaven as witness, I choose you, Mary, as my Mother and Queen. I surrender and consecrate myself to you, body and soul, with all that I possess, both spiritual and material, even including the spiritual value of all my actions, past, present, and to come. I give you the full right to dispose of me and all that belongs to me, without any reservations, in whatever way you please, for the greater glory of God, in time and throughout eternity.

Amen